WILLIAM &
CATHERINE

A Family Portrait

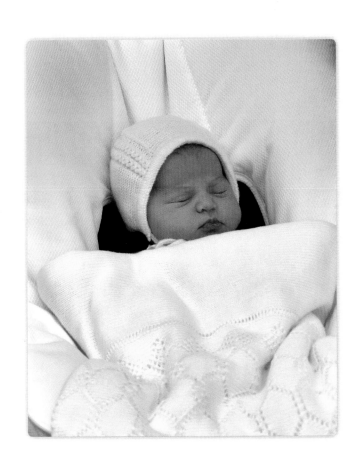

WILLIAM & CATHERINE

A Family Portrait

GILL KNAPPETT

PITKIN

Written by Gill Knappett.
The moral right of the author has been asserted.

Edited by Lindsey Smith.
Picture research by Gill Knappett and Lindsey Smith.
Cover designed by Katie Beard.
Designed by Glad Stockdale.

A CIP catalogue record for this book is available from the
British Library.

Published by Pitkin Publishing, The History Press, The Mill,
Brimscombe Port, Stroud, Gloucestershire GL5 2QG, UK
www.thehistorypress.co.uk

Printed in Great Britain.
ISBN 978-1-84165-642-7   1/15

CONTENTS

FOREWORD

A handsome prince whose destiny is to be Sovereign of the United Kingdom falls in love with a pretty girl from an ordinary, middle-class background. As William Shakespeare wrote in *The Tempest*, 'such stuff as dreams are made on'.

Prince William and Catherine Middleton's first meeting as students at St Andrews University led to a courtship and a love-match willed on by the world at large, including the Royal Family, who approved of this young woman with a quiet sense of discretion.

When they announced their engagement in November 2010, the nation rejoiced. The world, it seemed, went into a frenzy of excitement as plans were made for their wedding just five months later.

When Prince William married Catherine Middleton on 29 April 2011, royalists everywhere gave a collective cheer of joy, and perhaps a small sigh of relief, that the future king had chosen so well. The Duke and Duchess of Cambridge are a perfect match and prove that one's origins do not matter when love is involved.

This royal couple have captured the attention, and indeed the hearts, of the public in a way not seen since William's mother, the late Diana, Princess of Wales, arrived on the royal scene in 1981. They have accomplished this in a way that contrasts completely with the previous, more formal image of royalty, when the mere mention of their names would have been in hushed, reverential tones.

Below: William and Harry having fun with their mother, Princess Diana, at Thorpe Park in 1993.

William's good looks, boyish charm and self-deprecating sense of humour, twinned with Catherine's natural beauty and style, and her outgoing personality, generate an impression of modern royalty that is a winning combination of star quality and an approachable, common touch.

William's life has been mapped out from the moment he was born. As king-in-waiting, his schooling and career path have all been part of his ongoing education, preparing him for his role as future monarch. His wife's significantly different background has been a definite advantage. Her parents and siblings welcomed William warmly, and her stable family life gave him a glimpse of the kind of happiness he longed for, and no doubt hoped any future children of his would enjoy.

Catherine appeared to move seamlessly into the role she now plays in 'The Firm' – the name King George VI bestowed on the immediate Royal Family over 60 years ago. Since the early days of her name being linked romantically to Prince William, her every move, her demeanour and her choice of outfits has been under close scrutiny. Full credit goes to her that she has not faltered, rising with dignity and grace above the occasional knock from those overly keen for a 'scoop'.

Following their marriage, the world waited with bated breath to know when the young couple would start a family. Royal babies are often born in the first year of

Right: A few weeks before the arrival of her second baby, the Duchess of Cambridge attends the Turner Contemporary art gallery in Margate, Kent in March 2015.

marriage: The Queen gave birth to Prince Charles six days before her first wedding anniversary; Prince William arrived 11 months after his father and Lady Diana Spencer were married.

Of particular interest to many was the change in the Succession to the Crown Act 2013, stating that males born after 28 October 2011 would no longer have precedence over an elder sister in the line of succession. Another change to the Act means there is no longer a disqualification 'from succeeding to the Crown or from possessing it as a result of marrying a person of the Roman Catholic faith'.

It was suggested in some circles that the Duke and Duchess of Cambridge were perhaps delaying starting a family so that they could play their part in The Queen's Diamond Jubilee celebrations in 2012. With William's grandmother being only the second monarch in British history to reach this remarkable milestone – the first being Queen Victoria in 1897 – it was a busy year for the Royal Family.

William and Catherine enjoyed more than a year together as man and wife before, on 3 December 2012, a little more than 19 months after their marriage, the announcement came from St James's Palace: 'Their Royal Highnesses the Duke and Duchess of Cambridge are very pleased to announce that the Duchess of Cambridge is expecting a baby. The Queen, the Duke of Edinburgh, the Prince of Wales, the Duchess of Cornwall and Prince Harry and members of both families are delighted with the news.'

So began the next round of close media attention. The spotlight fell on Catherine as she suffered from acute morning sickness in the early months of pregnancy, resulting in a stay in hospital.

Below: As part of Queen Elizabeth II's Diamond Jubilee celebrations in 2012, the Duke and Duchess of Cambridge spent nine days on a royal tour of the Far East and South Pacific. Here in a Tuvalu village they drink from a coconut from a tree originally planted by The Queen.

As she recovered over the next few months, photographers were eager to snap her stylish choice of maternity outfits – and to capture a hint of her 'baby bump'.

Speculation was rife about when the child, who would be third in line to the throne, was due – and what he or she would be called. Royal officials said that the Duke and Duchess had 'decided not to find out' whether it was a boy or girl, but it was Catherine herself who let slip that the baby was due in mid-July.

Admitted to St Mary's Hospital, Paddington on the morning of Monday 22 July 2013, Catherine gave birth to a baby boy later that day. His arrival was great cause for celebration. The Duke, Duchess and their son left hospital the next day – and they did not keep everyone in suspense for much longer, as on 24 July his name was announced: George Alexander Louis.

Apart from a few, rare public appearances and official engagements – including a tour of New Zealand and Australia – Prince George's parents have their son out of the spotlight as much as possible. On the occasions he has been photographed, he is clearly a happy and much-loved little boy.

It is obvious to all who see them how much William and Catherine are enjoying parenthood. It was no surprise, therefore, when on 8 September 2014 it was announced that they were expecting their second child in the coming spring.

With the arrival of their daughter Charlotte on 2 May 2015, their family unit grew, and the nation rejoices at this latest addition to the Royal Family.

Right: The Duke and Duchess of Cambridge took great delight in having their son with them on their three-week tour of Australia and New Zealand in April 2014.

DATES AND EVENTS

1982   Catherine Middleton and Prince William are born: Miss Middleton at the Royal Berkshire Hospital, Reading, on 9 January; the Prince on 21 June at St Mary's Hospital, Paddington, London.

1991   The young Prince William undertakes an early public engagement when he accompanies his parents, Prince Charles and Princess Diana, on a visit to Llandaff Cathedral to celebrate St David's Day.

1995   Prince William, as 'William Wales', goes to Eton College in Berkshire. Catherine Middleton is a pupil at Marlborough College in Wiltshire.

2001   William and Catherine meet at St Andrews University, where they are both studying Art History; they have rooms close to each other in St Salvator's Hall.

2002   In March, William buys a £200 ticket to a charity fashion show and is impressed by Catherine's appearance on the catwalk.

2002   In their second year at university, William and Catherine flat share with other friends.

2003   In May, newspapers publish photographs of William and Catherine deep in conversation at a rugby match.

2003   Catherine is a guest at William's 21st birthday party at Windsor Castle; in September, with their flatmates, they move into a cottage for their third year at university.

2006   For the first time, Prince William is photographed kissing Catherine, during a skiing holiday at Klosters in January.

2006   In January, Prince William starts his army training at Sandhurst; in November, Catherine begins work as an accessories buyer for fashion chain Jigsaw.

2006   In December, Catherine is invited to Sandhurst to watch William graduate as an army officer.

2007   Prince William starts army training in Dorset. In April, it is confirmed that William and Catherine have split up, but by June it is rumoured that they are back together again.

2007   In October, the couple are photographed together and Catherine is invited to Balmoral for the weekend.

2008   In April, Catherine is at the Prince's side as he graduates from the RAF at Cranwell.

2008   In June, Catherine appears at a formal royal public occasion for the first time: to watch William take part in the Order of the Garter Service at Windsor Castle.

2010   In January, Catherine watches as William graduates from an advanced helicopter-flying course, receiving his wings from his father, the Prince of Wales.

2010   On 16 November, William and Catherine's engagement is announced.

2011   In February, William is made a Colonel in the Irish Guards. Catherine attends her first official engagement with her fiancé, naming a new lifeboat in Anglesey.

2011   In March, the couple make an official visit to Northern Ireland. A week later, the Prince pays an official visit to Australia and New Zealand.

2011   On 29 April, William and Catherine marry at Westminster Abbey.

2012   William, Catherine and Prince Harry are ambassadors for the 2012 Summer Olympics in London.

2012   On 3 December, an announcement from St James's Palace states that the Duke and Duchess of Cambridge are expecting their first child in the summer.

2013   On 5 June, William and Catherine join other members of the Royal Family and dignitaries in Westminster Abbey for a service marking the 60th anniversary of Queen Elizabeth II's coronation.

2013   George Alexander Louis, the new Prince of Cambridge, is born on 22 July, at St Mary's Hospital, Paddington, London.

2013   In September, Prince William leaves the RAF to spend more time on royal duties and charity work. Soon after he, Catherine and George move into their newly refurbished home at Kensington Palace.

2013   Prince George is baptised by the Archbishop of Canterbury at the Chapel Royal at St James's Palace on 23 October.

2014   It is announced that Prince William is to train as a helicopter pilot with East Anglian Air Ambulance, and confirmed that the family will make a second home in Norfolk.

2014   In April, eight-month-old Prince George accompanies his parents on a three-week official tour of New Zealand and Australia.

2014   On 8 September, Kensington Palace confirms that William and Catherine are expecting their second child in the spring.

2015   The Duke and Duchess of Cambridge's second child, Charlotte Elizabeth Diana, the new Princess of Cambridge, is born on 2 May, like her father and brother before her in the private Lindo Wing of St Mary's Hospital, Paddington, London.

A TWENTY-FIRST-CENTURY PRINCE

Early in the morning of 23 June 1982, a young father stood proudly on the steps outside St Mary's Hospital, Paddington. Prince Charles, heir to the throne, held his then unnamed child, just 36 hours old, who would also one day be king.

'The birth of our son has given us both more pleasure than you can imagine,' said a tired and delighted Prince Charles. 'It has made me incredibly proud and somewhat amazed.'

Prince William Arthur Philip Louis of Wales entered the world at 9.03 p.m. on 21 June in the private Lindo Wing of St Mary's Hospital. He was driven home to Kensington Palace, where he was to spend the next 16 years of his life.

> Prince William became the first 'heir presumptive' (an heir, other than the first in line to the throne) to be born in an ordinary hospital, albeit in an expensive private wing, rather than in a royal residence. This was seen by many as a sign that the young Prince was entering a changing world, far different from that occupied by his father in 1948.

Right: A proud Prince Charles carries the newborn William as he and Princess Diana leave hospital for their home at Kensington Palace.

William's mother, Princess Diana, was determined to be hands-on when it came to bringing up her children and, just a few weeks after his birth when she and Prince Charles left Britain for a long tour of Australia, she insisted that her child travel with her. If traditionalists criticised her 'modern' approach to rearing the heir presumptive, the rest of the world did not.

Far left: Six-month-old William sits propped against cushions at Kensington Palace.

Left: The Prince of Wales and Diana, Princess of Wales arrive with baby Prince William in Alice Springs, Australia in April 1983.

SCHOOLDAYS

Although a governess usually taught royal children at home until they were at least seven years old, Diana was keen that her son should escape the confines of the Palace and learn how to socialise with other children. William therefore started at a small private nursery school in Notting Hill Gate in September 1985. The transition from being the centre of attention of his nanny, Barbara Barnes, to one of many children at school was probably a hard lesson to learn, but has stood William in good stead.

Two years later he moved to the pre-preparatory Wetherby School, West London, where he enjoyed classroom activities and displayed an aptitude for sport. It was at this time that a new nanny, Ruth Wallace, arrived at Kensington Palace to teach her young charge not only self-reliance but also the importance of consideration and kindness to others.

Both William and, later, his younger brother Harry, became boarders at Ludgrove School in Berkshire, where William excelled at sport. He was tall for his age and soon became captain of both the rugby and hockey teams, and one of the school stars at clay pigeon shooting, having learned how to handle a gun from a very early age.

Left: Young William after his first day at nursery school, with a finger puppet he had made for his mother.

13

An early lesson that every member of the Royal Family has to learn is that they are forever in the public eye. One of William's first public engagements took place when, at just eight years old, he accompanied his parents on a visit to Llandaff Cathedral to celebrate St David's Day. With a daffodil in his buttonhole, a visit to the principality from which William takes his title was an appropriate baptism into public life. When the young Prince signed his name in the visitors' book at the cathedral, onlookers noticed that he is left-handed.

Another break with royal tradition came when the tough regime of Gordonstoun – the Scottish public school attended by William's grandfather, father and uncles – was eschewed in favour of Eton College. The first choice of both Diana and the Queen Mother, William was also pleased: friends from Ludgrove would be there, and the school was close to Windsor Castle where he could join his grandmother, The Queen, for Sunday tea.

'William Wales' first signed the Eton schoolbook in September 1995. In his small study-bedroom in Manor House, William stamped his own mark with a picture of Aston Villa (the football team he has always supported), a signed poster of All Saints (his favourite band at the time) and various other posters.

William excelled not only at football and rugby but also at swimming, becoming the 'Keeper of Swimming': Eton-speak for captain of the swimming team. He did well academically too, gaining three A-levels with grades good enough to win a place at St Andrews University in Scotland. But first he decided to see something of the world by taking a gap year.

Above: Prince William captaining his side (Gaileys) in his house colours of fawn and blue in the semi-final of an inter-house tournament between Gaileys and Hursts at Eton.

Anyone seeing the two young sons of Diana, Princess of Wales walking slowly, heads bowed, behind her funeral cortège on 6 September 1997 could not fail to be moved. The boys were at particularly vulnerable ages – William was 15 and Harry just two years younger – when their mother died in a tragic car accident in Paris. Despite the public outpouring of grief, the young brothers kept their emotions firmly under control, showing a maturity that belied their years.

William and Harry found security at their father's home, Highgrove, Gloucestershire, where Prince Charles coped admirably with their care after Princess Diana's death.

A GAP YEAR – AND UP TO UNIVERSITY

William's first destination was Belize in Central America, where he joined the Welsh Guards on exercise in the stifling hot and humid jungle. It was here that he first had an opportunity to use semi-automatic weapons.

In contrast, his second stop was the white sands and gentle breezes of Mauritius in the Indian Ocean. Under the name 'Brian Woods', William registered on the island of Rodrigues as a helper on a Royal Geographical Society marine conservation programme.

Chile came next, during the rainy season. The first week of this Raleigh International expedition saw torrential rain, day and night. 'Eventually even the tent became wet through; it was saturated . . . we became quite demoralised even though we somehow managed to keep ourselves going by singing, telling jokes and stories,' said William on his return.

When the rain stopped, the volunteers moved to the village of Tortel, teaching English to the children and making friends with the locals.

William took in his stride the variety of experiences during his gap year: his early domestic life had often been one of contrasts and he was used to discomforts as well as the comforts

Below: Prince William wearing his own choice of waistcoat as a member of 'Pop', Eton's small group of prefects. Pop originated in 1811 as a debating society which met in Mrs Hatton's Lollipop Shop, on which School Hall now stands.

Right: Prince William helped construct walkways linking buildings in the village of Tortel, Southern Chile during his Raleigh International expedition.

William's grandmother, Her Majesty Queen Elizabeth II, laid down a few ground rules for William at university. These were: no smoking, only moderate drinking and certainly no drugs. If he dated a woman he was never to be seen kissing her in public. Nor was he ever to ask his bodyguard to leave him alone, even at private parties. The last was a rule that William had been observing since he was old enough to understand the ways of the world: never discuss any member of the Royal Family, even with those to whom he had become close.

afforded an heir to the royal throne. At home – Highgrove, St James's Palace in London, Balmoral in Scotland or Sandringham in Norfolk – his clothes would be laid out by a valet and he would be woken each morning by a footman bearing a 'calling tray' with coffee and biscuits. But there had been no such luxuries at Eton; nor were there at St Andrews University where, in September 2001, William Wales joined 6,000 other students.

William changed his university subject from Art History to Geography and achieved a Scottish Master of Arts degree with upper second class honours – the highest university honours gained by an heir to the British throne.

A GRADUATE PRINCE

Sometime in the future Prince William will be crowned king. While he waits, as his father has done for several decades, he has carved a career path and become accustomed to duties.

William has a strong sense of duty, instilled in him by his Windsor forebears. He takes a keen interest in charitable causes, many of them once supported by his mother, Princess Diana. In 1996 Diana took William and his brother Harry on visits to Centrepoint, the charity for young homeless people she supported. William later took on patronage of Centrepoint and proved his commitment to raising awareness of the cause by sleeping rough near Blackfriars Bridge one freezing December night in 2009.

William is also patron or president of a number of other charities and organisations in the UK and abroad. Sport remains high on his agenda and, reflecting his schoolboy sporting passions, he has been President of England's Football Association since 2006, patron of the English Schools' Swimming Association since 2007, patron of the Welsh Rugby Charitable Trust since 2012, and since 2014 has been President of the British Sub-Aqua Club.

After leaving university William settled on a career in the armed forces, graduating from Sandhurst in December 2006. Lieutenant William Wales followed his brother Harry into the Blues and Royals as a troop commander in an armoured reconnaissance unit. His wish to see active service was

Below: Graduates, including Prince William, march in the Sovereign's Parade at Sandhurst, December 2006.

Right: Prince William is greeted warmly in a flood-hit farming region in southern Australia during a visit to disaster zones there and in New Zealand in 2011.

In 2009 Princes William and Harry created The Foundation to support issues close to their hearts. In 2011 they were joined by Catherine, and The Foundation was renamed The Royal Foundation of The Duke and Duchess of Cambridge and Prince Harry, focusing on three main areas: the armed forces, young people and conservation.

discouraged, so William trained in both the Royal Navy and the Royal Air Force. Four months of intensive training at Cranwell won him his RAF wings, presented to him in April 2008 at a ceremony watched by Catherine Middleton.

William served as a helicopter pilot with the RAF's Search and Rescue Force, based with No. 22 Squadron at RAF Valley on Anglesey, until September 2013, when he left operational service to increasingly support his grandmother in an official capacity. He has since trained to become a helicopter pilot with East Anglian Air Ambulance, based at Cambridge and Norwich Airports. Initially a co-pilot, since spring 2015 he has flown on day and night shifts and will ultimately qualify as a helicopter commander.

Above: Harry, William and Catherine during a visit to Bacon's College, London in July 2012 to launch a programme involving The Royal Foundation of the Duke and Duchess of Cambridge and Prince Harry, in partnership with the Greenhouse Sports charity.

Left: Prince William escorts his grandmother during Her Majesty's visit to RAF Valley at Holyhead in April 2011, during his time there as a search and rescue helicopter pilot.

William's full title is Prince William of Wales KG KT. KG stands for Knight of the Garter and he became the 1,000th Knight when he was installed on 15 June 2008 at the Annual Garter Ceremony at Windsor Castle. KT stands for Knight of the Order of the Thistle, an honour bestowed on him on 29 May 2012 in The Queen's Diamond Jubilee year.

On his 21st birthday William became a Counsellor of State, in place of Princess Anne. Counsellors of State carry out some of The Queen's official duties in her absence. Current Counsellors of State are the Duke of Edinburgh and the four adults next in the line of succession, aged 21 or over: Prince Charles, Prince William, Prince Harry and Prince Andrew.

A DUCHESS IN THE MAKING

Catherine Elizabeth Middleton was born at the Royal Berkshire Hospital, Reading, on 9 January 1982, making her just five months older than Prince William. Who would have guessed that this baby, born to an ordinary family, would one day marry a prince?

FAMILY VALUES

Catherine is, in royal parlance, 'a commoner', a middle-class woman from a wealthy, self-made family with loving parents who gave her every advantage educationally and socially. She is well mannered without being stuffy, charming without being precious, good-tempered and accommodating but with a will and mind of her own, qualities that clearly endear her to the British public.

In the years before William and Catherine's engagement, she, her parents and siblings passed the 'loyalty test', never letting slip any details about the relationship. Catherine had to behave as discreetly as a royal even then, and her family – especially her mother Carole and sister Pippa – gave, and continue to give, her great comfort and support.

On her mother's side Catherine is descended from a line of Durham miners. Her maternal grandfather, Ron Goldsmith, left school at 14 and eventually established a building business in Southall, West London. His daughter Carole, Catherine's mother, joined BOAC (British Overseas Airways Corporation – now British Airways) as cabin crew and, during the 1970s, met and married Michael Middleton.

Mr Middleton grew up in Leeds where his father, a pilot, came from forebears who were solicitors, mill owners and minor landowners. Michael, for a while cabin crew with BOAC, trained as a pilot before working in airline administration.

Below: Catherine Middleton, together with her sister Pippa and her mother Carole, acknowledges the crowd outside The Goring Hotel in London on the day before her marriage to William in 2011.

Marlborough College, founded in 1843 by the Church of England for the sons of impoverished clergy, is built around a pretty Queen Anne house on rolling Wiltshire downland. It has educated some of Britain's most prominent women, among them Princess Eugenie of York, Emily Sheffield (deputy editor of *Vogue*), writer Lauren Child (creator of the Charlie and Lola books) and designer Antonia Robinson.

AN ADMIRABLE STUDENT

It was after the birth of their third child, James, that Carole Middleton spotted a gap in the market and set up a business selling costumes, toys, games and novelties for various types of parties. The success of the family business, now run from a large barn at their Berkshire home in Bucklebury, enabled Catherine's parents to give her a privileged education, sending her first to St Andrew's School in Pangbourne and then to Marlborough College, where Catherine justified the £29,000 annual fee by becoming an admirable student.

At Marlborough Catherine met the children of the rich and famous but, like all Marlburiennes, she learnt how to be fair and tough. Schoolfriends remember her as an initially shy girl who transformed into a confident, outgoing teenager, hard-working, athletic, popular and level-headed. On her journey to achieving three good A-levels, including A grades for Maths and Art, Catherine became head of her house, Elmhurst, captain of the school hockey team, and was known for her dependability and loyalty. She had all the qualities, in fact, of a perfect modern princess.

Like Prince William, Catherine opted for a gap year before going on to St Andrews University to study Art History. She too spent time working on a project in Chile, also visiting the Caribbean and Florence.

Left: Catherine and her siblings, Pippa and James, all attended Marlborough College in Wiltshire.

By the time Catherine arrived at Marlborough, once a boys-only college, girls were a fixture. When the first female students were admitted in 1968 the prospect of being watched and 'marked' by dozens of boys was a daunting one, but it was character-forming. 'Anything after walking across court for the first time, watched by all those boys, is a piece of cake,' said one former pupil.

UNIVERSITY AND BEYOND

When Catherine Middleton went up to St Andrews University, in the small Scottish town of the same name, she was not the only pupil there from Marlborough College. Some of her former schoolmates knew Prince William, so it was not long before he and Catherine were on friendly terms – although she admits she felt embarrassed when they were first introduced: 'I actually think I went bright red and sort of scuttled off, feeling very shy,' she revealed.

Below: Catherine at her graduation ceremony, St Andrews University, June 2005.

Left: Catherine enjoys a day at the horse trials at Gatcombe Park in Gloucestershire, August 2005.

Below: Catherine takes part in a training session for a charity rowing event in June 2007.

Left: William and Catherine on their first official engagement as a couple: the naming of a new lifeboat at Trearddur Bay Lifeboat Station on Anglesey, February 2011.

Catherine graduated from St Andrews with a 2:1 in Art History. She started a career in the fashion business, becoming an accessories buyer for the high street clothes chain Jigsaw. Fashion-conscious Kate's post-university style was generally jeans or casual trousers tucked into long leather boots, teamed with a blouse or jacket, and she was often spotted wearing Jigsaw clothes, along with other stylish brands such as L.K. Bennett, Kew and Whistles.

A change of career came when her parents' company needed a marketing manager. In 2007 she decided to work at promoting the family business back home in rural Berkshire.

That all had to stop when she became William's fiancée. She handed over projects such as designing the Christmas catalogue, arranging press coverage for the thriving company, organising photo shoots and visiting trade fairs to others; suddenly her job was to become a member of the Royal Family.

Right: Catherine at the wedding of William's close friend Nicholas van Custem to Alice Hadden-Paton at The Guards Chapel, Wellington Barracks, London in August 2009.

FROM STUDENTS TO SWEETHEARTS

By the end of freshers' week 2001 at St Andrews University, Catherine Middleton had been dubbed the prettiest girl at 'Sallies' (St Salvator's Hall).

Both she and Prince William were enrolled on the same course, and soon they were meeting over breakfast, served in the grand dining hall with portraits of Scottish philosophers lined up above them on the walls. They had a love of the countryside, sporting pursuits and swimming in common. By coincidence their gap years had followed a similar pattern and Catherine was able to talk about the Renaissance art she had seen in Florence and which would feature on the Art History course.

But talking was all that happened at this stage; they both had romantic liaisons with other people during their first term, though Catherine's name was never linked to any other serious boyfriend.

However, when William realised that his chosen course was not for him, chats with – and a growing interest in – the pretty chestnut-haired student, who seemed quieter and more sympathetic than many of the others, helped his decision to switch his studies to Geography.

There is no forgetting the Prince's reaction to Catherine's appearance in the annual charity fashion show at a St Andrews hotel during their second term at university. He paid £200 for a front-row seat and was bowled over when his friend Catherine sashayed down the catwalk in a sheer shift dress. 'Wow!' was his response. The dress, designed by Charlotte Todd, was later sold at auction for thousands of pounds.

Although Catherine might have welcomed his attention, she wisely kept the attraction she and the young Prince were feeling for each other low key, and let matters develop slowly.

Below: The quadrangle at St Salvator's Hall where William and Catherine first met.

William recalled the early days: 'We were friends for over a year first and it just sort of blossomed. We just spent more time with each other, had a good giggle, lots of fun, and realised we shared the same interests and had a really good time.'

By the time they went up for their second year, William and Catherine had become part of a group of four friends sharing a flat in St Andrews town centre, fitted out with bullet-proof windows, bomb-proof doors and a sophisticated laser security system. If they were romantically linked they managed to keep things discreet, never touching or holding hands in public, and arriving at parties separately.

To the world and the sharp-eyed press, they were just good friends.

When William's 21st birthday was celebrated with a party at Windsor Castle in June 2003, it is likely that he and Catherine were in a relationship, although the Prince denied that he had a steady girlfriend.

They were close enough during their third and final years at university to share a secluded cottage, establishing a cosy domesticity, but still managing to keep the relationship a secret. Their tight circle of friends helped, never breaking the code of silence that bound them to the young couple. Through all this, Catherine was discretion itself, careful not to be seen in any compromising situation with William.

St Andrews has a reputation as a university for forging long-lasting relationships. At William and Catherine's graduation ceremony in June 2005, the university's vice-chancellor Dr Brian Lang uttered words that many have seen as prophetic: 'You will have made lifelong friends,' he told the young people seated in front of him. 'You may have met your husband or wife. Our title as the top match-making university in Britain signifies so much that is good about St Andrews, so we rely on you to go forth and multiply.'

Right: Catherine caught Prince William's eye when she modelled in a student fashion show at St Andrews in March 2002.

Right: Catherine Middleton, flanked by her father Michael and her mother Carole, is an invited guest at Prince William's passing out parade at the Royal Military Academy, Sandhurst in December 2006.

In 2004 the pair were spotted on the slopes enjoying a skiing holiday together at Klosters in Switzerland, and the secret was out in the open. Once they left university, William had to fulfil his royal duties and forge his career, the press never far away. No one had seen them behaving like lovers, but they were often spotted together and when Catherine moved into a flat in central London with an old friend from her boarding-school days, she found the full glare of the media spotlight on her private life.

Catherine coped admirably, resigned to the fact that she would have to dress carefully, wear make-up and be suitably coiffured every time she stepped outside in order to face the photographers lying in wait. She kept a low profile at major events. She was not seen at the marriage of Prince Charles and Camilla Parker Bowles in 2005, although she did attend other weddings with William that year.

Left: Catherine was a guest at Prince William's graduation from Cranwell in April 2008, joining members of the Royal Family for the occasion.

As friendship turned slowly to love, the many ways that the couple were well suited became apparent. William, the handsome young man who will one day be king, could have had his pick of European princesses and aristocratic young women for his bride. But his heart was captured by an ordinary, although extraordinarily attractive, girl from the Home Counties – indicating that William is unpretentious and listens to his own feelings rather than trying to satisfy convention. In Catherine he found a woman with whom he feels comfortable: sporty and sharing his love of the outdoor life (a must for anyone joining the Royal Family), cheerful, resourceful, uncomplicated and creative. They both display a sense of fun: 'She's got a really naughty sense of humour, which kind of helps me, because I've got a really dry sense of humour. We had a good laugh – and things happened,' he said.

Although William continued to deny that marriage was in the air, their relationship was widely accepted, especially after he was photographed kissing Catherine on another Klosters holiday in 2006. It seemed too that the Royal Family had accepted her as William's girlfriend when images of William and his father, happy and at ease in her company, were circulated in the press.

Pressure from William's life in the forces was blamed for the couple's brief separation in early spring 2007 – but within weeks they were back together again as if nothing had happened.

From 2007 Catherine appeared at a number of high-profile events, including the Princes' Concert for Diana, where she was a VIP guest in the royal box, and William's 'Wings' presentation ceremony in April 2008. She was also invited to the wedding of Peter Phillips, The Queen's grandson. This was the occasion where she first met The Queen. And in June 2008 she was asked to St George's Chapel, Windsor Castle, where she watched William's investiture into the Order of the Garter.

Left: Catherine Middleton, Prince Harry and the Duchess of Cornwall attend the Garter Ceremony at Windsor Castle to see Prince William invested as a Knight of the Garter, June 2008.

THE ENGAGEMENT

Catherine Middleton waited a long time for her prince. Her romance with Prince William was slow-burning and took eight years to reach its joyous denouement. The announcement from Clarence House, just after 11 o'clock on Tuesday 16 November 2010, was matter-of-fact, but its joyful impact was felt by a nation hungry for a genuine love story.

There could be no doubt in anyone's mind that this was the real thing. Catherine Middleton took Prince William's arm as they walked into the red and gold grandeur of the Entrée Room at St James's Palace to face the world's media. Love shone through every gesture and exchanged glance as the young couple told of their happiness and plans for the future.

Right: Prince William and Catherine Middleton announce their engagement amid the grandeur of St James's Palace.

Catherine, facing her first formal public appearance with her royal fiancé and admitting that the prospect of joining the Royal Family was a daunting one, emerged with credit from this debut.

When William and Catherine shared their happy news with a delighted world, no one could have failed to notice the beautiful sapphire, surrounded by 14 brilliant-cut diamonds, set in a white-gold band on the third finger of her perfectly manicured left hand.

Catherine's oval engagement ring is of more than usual emotional significance to the couple. It was the ring given to the Prince's mother, then Lady Diana Spencer, by Prince Charles when he proposed 29 years previously.

Why did William wait such a long time to propose to the woman who is clearly the love of his life? Having been close to William for several years before their engagement, Catherine had some idea of the constant pressure they would both be under. On the day they became engaged William told the world that he had waited so long to ask her to be his wife because he knew the pressure of royal life was daunting and he wanted to give Catherine the opportunity to see 'what happens on the other side'. 'I wanted to give her the chance to see and to back out if she needed to, before it all got too much,' he said.

The Queen admitted her joy at the 'brilliant' news. Prince Charles, too, said he was thrilled and, in a characteristic display of dry humour, added: 'They've been practising long enough.' William's stepmother, the Duchess of Cornwall, was clearly delighted. She told reporters: 'I'm just so happy and so are they. It's wicked!'

Left: Catherine's engagement ring holds special memories. The beautiful sapphire, surrounded by 14 brilliant-cut diamonds and set in a white-gold band, was given to William's mother, Princess Diana, on her engagement to Prince Charles.

'It's very special to me,' William told the world as cameras homed in on the sparkling ring, which fitted Catherine perfectly without alteration. 'Kate is very special to me now … It was my way of making sure that my mother didn't miss out on today, and the excitement and the fact that we're going to spend the rest of our lives together.'

When William and Catherine flew out to Kenya in October 2010, she had no idea that this was anything more than a holiday to see spectacular wildlife and to enjoy time together in the seclusion of the African bush. Yet tucked away in William's rucksack was the ring which he planned to put on Catherine's finger if she agreed to become his wife.

Just before their holiday was due to end, William drove Catherine to the shores of the Rutundu Lake, high on the slopes of Mount Kenya, where the couple stayed in a romantic wooden lodge. Here the Prince asked Catherine to be his wife, and she accepted. Neither revealed any details of the proposal. Catherine would only say: 'It was very romantic and it was very personal.'

Many royal marriages are arranged to unite two nations, or as a marriage of convenience between two families eager to strengthen their ties by such a union. William and Catherine made sure their marriage would be different. They were the prime movers and they made decisions on their own terms. It is clear that they were marrying for love, and with a great deal of friendship and goodwill on both sides.

William revealed that he did ask Michael Middleton for his daughter's hand in marriage – but he waited until she had accepted his proposal: 'I was torn between asking Kate's father first and then the realisation that he might actually say "no" dawned. So I thought, "If I ask Kate first, he can't really say no". So I did it that way.'

Catherine's warm and happy family welcomed Prince William into their home without fuss or pretension, never boasting to the neighbours or letting slip details about the relationship to the media. That discretion and Catherine's own stood her in good stead, winning the approval of William's grandmother, The Queen.

Patience, too, is a virtue, and certainly a quality Catherine displayed when she and William were playing the 'waiting game'. During the many times that William was away on royal duties, family holidays or undergoing periods of training and service with the armed forces, Catherine showed that she was prepared to stay at home without fuss. Catherine's future in-laws clearly noted these qualities and gave Catherine the royal 'thumbs up'. Prince William could not have chosen a better wife.

Catherine knew that in marrying Prince William she was, in a way, marrying the whole nation. Although already carrying out public duties, when he succeeds to the throne William will be subjected to an almost daily round of functions, and she will be at his side.

Prince William's wife was known to the world as 'Kate', but after her marriage she chose to use the more formal version of her name. On her husband's eventual succession to the throne she will become the sixth Queen Catherine, following Henry V's wife Catherine of Valois (d. 1437), three wives of Henry VIII – Catherine of Aragon (d. 1536), Catherine Howard (beheaded 1542) and Catherine Parr (d. 1548) – and later, Catherine of Braganza, who married Charles II in 1662.

Left: A loving glance between the happy couple tells of their joy on the day they announced their engagement.

THE
ROYAL WEDDING

W hen the Great Door of Westminster Abbey was ceremoniously opened early on the morning of 29 April 2011, guests were already lining up to celebrate the wedding of His Royal Highness Prince William of Wales KG and Miss Catherine Middleton, the 16th royal couple to be married in the Abbey.

Well-wishers from all walks of life filled every available space along the route from Clarence House, Buckingham Palace and the Goring Hotel, many waving the Union Jack on this most British of occasions.

Below: Prince William and his best man and brother, Prince Harry, are happy and at ease as they enter Westminster Abbey.

THE GROOM, BEST MAN AND GUESTS

As guests such as David and Victoria Beckham, Sir Elton John, Governors-General and Prime Ministers were shown to their seats, a burst of cheering outside announced the arrival of a Bentley bearing the bridegroom – William, newly made Duke of Cambridge, resplendent in his scarlet uniform of Colonel of the Irish Guards – and his best man, his brother, Prince Harry, wearing his formal Blues and Royals officer's uniform.

They made their way into the Abbey, stopping to greet their uncle, Charles Spencer, the ninth Earl Spencer, brother of their late mother, before being escorted to St Edmund's Chapel.

The Very Reverend Dr John Hall, Dean of Westminster, greeted the parents of the bride and bridegroom. Carole Middleton – wearing a Catherine Walker pale blue silk dress with a blue wool crêpe coat – arrived first, accompanied by her 23-year-old son, James.

Their Royal Highnesses the Duke and Duchess of Cornwall stepped out of a 1950 Rolls Royce Phantom, she wearing a champagne silk dress designed by Anna Valentine with a matching hand-embroidered coat.

A fanfare by the State Trumpeters of the Household Cavalry rang out to announce Her Majesty The Queen and His Royal Highness Prince Philip, the last members of the Royal Family to arrive. Designer Angela Kelly was responsible for Her Majesty's primrose yellow crêpe wool outfit, and hat trimmed with silk roses and leaves.

HERE COMES THE BRIDE

The Rolls Royce Phantom VI carrying Catherine and her father drew to a halt outside the great church and the bride stepped out, revealing to the world the dress that had remained a secret until this moment: and it was perfect.

The ivory lace and satin wedding dress exceeded the expectations of the fashion critics. It was deliciously simple in shape, but a world of craftsmanship, design and expertise had gone into its making by a team led by designer Sarah Burton of British fashion house Alexander McQueen.

Right: The bride, her father and attendants, led by the Dean of Westminster, process slowly up the aisle to the High Altar and the awaiting Prince William.

Below: Catherine exchanges a smile with her sister and maid of honour, Pippa Middleton, as they prepare to walk into the Abbey for the wedding service. Pippa is holding the train, almost three metres (nine feet) long.

The skirt evoked an opening flower, the bodice was finished at the back with 58 tiny satin-covered buttons, and the underskirt was trimmed with English Cluny lace. The design incorporated appliquéd English and Chantilly lace, each piece hand-cut in the shape of a flower – the English rose, Scottish thistle, Welsh daffodil and Irish shamrock – and stitched on to the dress and the train using the ancient Carrickmacross lacemaking technique.

Catherine's bridal veil, decorated with hand-embroidered flowers, was held in place by a Cartier 'halo' tiara, loaned to the bride by The Queen, a gift to celebrate Her Majesty's 18th birthday. Catherine's earrings were a wedding present from her parents; based on their new family crest the design incorporated diamond-set stylised oak leaves and acorns.

The only adult attendant, Catherine's sister Philippa (Pippa) was maid of honour and looked stunning in a dress by Sarah Burton of ivory satin-based crêpe with a cowl front. Pippa gathered the train of the exquisite bridal gown, while the small bridesmaids and pageboys clustered around excitedly.

The four young bridesmaids – Lady Louise Windsor, seven, the Hon. Margarita Armstrong-Jones, eight, and three-year-olds Grace van Cutsem and Eliza Lopes – wore ballerina-length dresses with full skirts, made by children's-wear designer Nicki Macfarlane. Each wore wreaths of lily of the valley and ivy in her hair, and carried small bouquets.

The pageboys – Billy Lowther-Pinkerton, ten, and Tom Pettifer, eight – wore uniforms featuring Irish shamrocks and the Harp of Ireland, influenced by the Irish Guards for whom Prince William was made Colonel in 2011.

THE CEREMONY

Catherine Middleton, a radiant and beautiful bride, her hand clasped firmly in her father's, stood for a few seconds in the light-filled space just inside the Great West Door of Westminster Abbey.

Her transformation from commoner to Duchess began as she walked along a crimson carpet marking the length of the nave and the quire to the sanctuary. Leading was the Dean of Westminster, while the choir sang *I Was Glad*, written by Charles Hubert Hastings Parry from Psalm 122. A fresh green avenue of trees and informal arrangements of white spring flowers along the nave and around the High Altar tempered the high majesty of the occasion.

Prince William, waiting for his bride, turned towards her only as she arrived at his side, and whispered, 'You look beautiful'. To Michael Middleton he joked, 'And this was supposed to be a small family affair.'

The couple, prompted by the Archbishop of Canterbury, the Most Reverend and Right Honourable Dr Rowan Williams, made their vows and the groom slipped the Welsh gold wedding ring on to his bride's finger.

After an address by the Lord Bishop of London, the Right Reverend and Right Honourable Dr Richard Chartres, a prayer prepared by William and Catherine, and the sole reading from Romans 12 given by Catherine's brother, the couple moved to the chapel of St Edward the Confessor to sign the registers confirming their status as man and wife.

The newly made Duchess of Cambridge bowed to her grandmother-in-law, The Queen, before walking back down the aisle, hand-in-hand with her husband, the Duke.

The couple started married life with three new titles each. In addition to the titles of Duke and Duchess of Cambridge, Her Majesty The Queen made William Earl of Strathearn and Baron Carrickfergus. Catherine, in turn, became Countess of Strathearn and Baroness Carrickfergus.

Left: William and Catherine leave Westminster Abbey after their marriage.

Left: Prince William holds his wife's wedding flowers as she is helped from the carriage by a footman on their arrival at Buckingham Palace.

ON TO THE CELEBRATIONS

The Abbey bells rang out as William and Catherine emerged into the spring sunshine to be greeted by the jubilant crowds.

The five-strong carriage procession with its two mounted escorts that bore the newly-weds, in the 1902 State Lanau, was British pageantry at its best. As the procession drew up outside Buckingham Palace, the Royal Standard fluttered aloft and 101 men from the 1st Battalion Welsh Guards formed a Guard of Honour. Prince William had brought his bride safely home.

The crowd waited for what has become a traditional highlight of all royal weddings: the appearance of the Royal Family on Buckingham Palace's balcony. William and Catherine emerged, soon joined by the rest of the wedding party. Then the happy couple kissed – twice – delighting the roaring crowd.

A fly-past was followed by The Queen's reception at the Palace, where 650 guests sipped champagne and tucked into a wonderful meal. Partying went on into the night, as Prince

Below: The Duke and Duchess of Cambridge take centre stage as the wedding party gathers in the Throne Room of Buckingham Palace.

Left: The newly married couple share a kiss on the balcony of Buckingham Palace.

Charles hosted a dinner dance for more than 300 guests at the Palace, ending with a spectacular fireworks display.

As thousands of people around Britain celebrated the royal wedding, millions more around the world followed the pageant on television. It was a glorious occasion of pomp and ceremony, and remembered as a day that united the nation in friendship and love. For the happy couple, they well knew their commitment to each other was one that also reflected their commitment to the nation as they prepared to fulfil an increasing number of royal duties.

2012: A Year of Celebrations

Britain celebrated two particularly significant events in 2012: The Queen's Diamond Jubilee and the London 2012 Olympics.

The nation was awash with excitement at the prospect of the Olympic Games being held here – the first time since 1948. The Duke and Duchess of Cambridge and Prince Harry were heavily involved with London 2012, as official ambassadors for Team GB and Paralympic GB, promoting Britain's athletes throughout the build-up as well as during the Olympic and Paralympic Games themselves.

At a gala dinner at the Royal Albert Hall in May, William had spoken to Olympians and Paralympians of his excitement at the prospect of the Games: 'We will witness an exceptional moment in our island's history. The mood in London will be electric, ecstatic and amazing. I simply can't wait.'

He was not disappointed. He, Catherine and Harry were present at many events, including the magnificent opening and closing ceremonies on 27 July and 12 August respectively, both of which were spectacular and will live on in the memories of all who experienced them for many years to come.

Celebrating a Diamond Jubilee is a remarkable achievement and Queen Elizabeth II is only the second monarch in British history to rule for 60 years. Commemorative events were held throughout the Commonwealth in 2012, though unlike her Silver and Golden Jubilees, The Queen and the Duke of Edinburgh toured only the United Kingdom. Other parts of the Commonwealth were visited by her children and grandchildren as her representatives William and Catherine took a nine-day tour of South East Asia and the South Pacific in September, when they visited Singapore, Malaysia, the Solomon Islands and Tuvalu.

Later in the year, on 30 November 2012, St Andrew's Day, the Duchess of Cambridge visited St Andrew's School in Pangbourne, Berkshire, where she studied from 1986 until 1995. Formally opening a new playing field, she participated in an impromptu game of hockey. Despite wearing high-heeled boots, her sporting prowess was once more at the fore and no one watching would have guessed she was carrying a secret soon to be revealed to the world: that she was pregnant.

The announcement came just three days later, after Catherine was taken to

Right: William and Catherine at the National Orchid Garden in Singapore, September 2012.

King Edward VII Hospital in central London suffering from acute and debilitating morning sickness. Although Catherine was not yet 12 weeks pregnant, the couple decided to go public with the news in view of her admission to hospital. A statement from the Palace advised: 'As the pregnancy is in its very early stages, Her Royal Highness is expected to stay in hospital for several days and will require a period of rest thereafter.' Prime Minister David Cameron spoke for the nation when he said, 'It's absolutely wonderful news and I'm sure everyone around the country will be celebrating with them tonight.'

Catherine's official visit to her old school in November 2012 was just one of many she and William would undertake both together and separately. One of their first trips as man and wife had been in July 2011 when they visited Canada on behalf of The Queen, receiving a warm welcome and enjoying Canada Day celebrations.

During the Duchess of Cambridge's visit to her old school, St Andrew's in Pangbourne, Deputy Head Richard Hudson revealed that Catherine still held the record at the school for the high jump.

2013:
AN EVENTFUL YEAR

For William and Catherine, the arrival of Prince George was, naturally, the highlight of 2013. Whilst they waited for the refurbishment of their London home at Kensington Palace to be completed, the couple lived on site in a small cottage. In October, the work was finished and the three of them moved in to their four-storey, 20-room family home: Apartment 1A, previously the home of The Queen's younger sister, Princess Margaret, who died in 2002.

The months preceding George's birth were busy for the royal couple. Although Catherine had to cancel some engagements when she was unwell, when she was out and about there was no outward sign of her pregnancy for quite some time.

When Catherine became Duchess, she took on a number of charity patronages in areas reflecting her particular interests. With her degree in Art History, Catherine has chosen to be involved with charities such as The Art Room, which uses art therapy to help children with emotional and behavioural difficulties, and the National Portrait Gallery.

In January 2013, Catherine, wearing an empire-line dress from Whistles, arrived with William at the National Portrait Gallery to view her new portrait by award-winning artist Paul Emsley. The head and shoulders portrait, using a technique of layers of oil and glazes, shines out of a dark background, and, at Catherine's suggestion, is a reflection of her natural rather than her official personae.

On 4 June 2013, The Queen and the Duke of Edinburgh, along with other members of the Royal Family and a 2,000-strong congregation, attended a service at Westminster Abbey to

Right: One 13 June 2013, Catherine made her last public appearance before the birth of Prince George when she named the *Royal Princess* cruise ship at Southampton.

mark the 60th anniversary of Her Majesty's coronation. Many eyes, however, were on the Duchess of Cambridge; in her pretty beige lace dress and matching coat, there was now no disguising the fact that she was eight months pregnant.

Catherine's first solo engagement post-baby came on 18 October when, as part of her involvement with SportsAid, she joined Olympians and Paralympians playing sports with young athletes in London's Olympic Park. Her trim figure belied the fact that she had given birth just months earlier, and she delighted her audience with several good shots in a game of volleyball, despite wearing high wedge-heeled shoes.

The previous month had been all change for William for he left his job as an RAF search and rescue pilot on Anglesey and commenced a series of royal engagements and projects with various charities and public bodies.

Below: The Duke and Duchess of Cambridge meet artist Paul Emsley after viewing his new portrait of the Duchess during a private viewing at the National Portrait Gallery in January 2013.

Catherine appeared in public only occasionally during the first few months following George's birth. She was first seen in August, when she and William started the Ring O'Fire Anglesey Coastal Ultra Marathon – a 135-mile run circumnavigating the island, their home territory at the time. Catherine told the crowd, eager for news of George, that her mother was on babysitting duty and that he was 'doing very well'.

Far left: New mum Catherine, a patron of SportsAid, plays volleyball during her visit to Olympic Park in October 2013.

Left: The Duke and Duchess of Cambridge speak with the Dean of Westminster Abbey, John Hall, as they leave the Abbey following a service of celebration to mark the 60th anniversary of Queen Elizabeth II's coronation.

THE BIRTH OF
PRINCE GEORGE

The long-awaited news that Catherine, accompanied by her husband, had checked into the exclusive private wing of St Mary's Hospital – where William was born 31 years earlier – turned a hot Monday in July into a day of fevered expectation for the British people. She and William, who stayed with her during the birth, had managed to give most of the hundreds of waiting journalists and photographers the slip by using a side entrance when they arrived in the early hours of the morning.

And so it was that on Monday 22 July 2013, the hottest day of the year, George Alexander Louis, the new Prince of Cambridge, was born in the air-conditioned private Lindo Wing of St Mary's Hospital, at 4.24 in the afternoon, weighing 8lbs 6oz. His parents, knowing they would have little privacy once the birth was made public, wanted to share those first precious hours alone with him. They managed to delay the long-awaited announcement until 8.30 that evening, when the nation and the world rejoiced.

The miracle of new life swept away memories of a long and tiring labour. The couple, sitting closely together, most likely wanted nothing more than to gaze at, touch and hold their baby

Far left: Catherine with her newborn son, about whom William joked, 'He's got her looks, thankfully.'

Left: William, Catherine and George leave St Mary's Hospital.

Far left: Michael and Carole Middleton were the first visitors to meet their new grandson.

Left: The Prince of Wales arrives with wife Camilla, Duchess of Cornwall to see the newest member of their family.

boy. The three of them were now a family and this was a private time to be savoured. But the new parents, aware that this was no ordinary birth, knew that their peaceful interlude could not last. As they and their baby got to know each other, the pressure of public expectation outside the hospital room was growing by the minute.

While Catherine and William marvelled at the fierce rush of protective love that takes all new parents by surprise, the world waited, impatient for news of this baby, one day to be king, a child destined to live his whole life with the eyes of the public upon him.

Breaking with royal tradition, an official notification of the birth was given to the press by an email sent from Kensington Palace. Only then was the framed foolscap bulletin, detailing

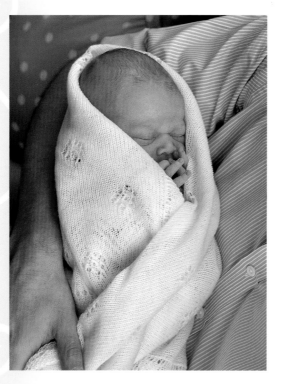

the time of birth and the baby's weight, delivered to Buckingham Palace through the Privy Purse door, before being fixed to an ornate gold-painted easel by The Queen's communications secretary, Aisla Anderson, helped by a liveried footman. The easel stood on Buckingham Palace's forecourt, just inside the railings. In another nod to the modern age, Clarence House then tweeted the details on Twitter.

The humid evening air outside Buckingham Palace crackled with excitement as a large and growing crowd pressed forward to take photographs of the historic document, signed by surgeon-gynaecologist Marcus Setchel who had delivered the new Prince. Even he was moved by the birth, murmuring 'wonderful baby, beautiful baby' as he left the Lindo Wing that evening.

Tourists and Londoners, excited visitors and those who rushed to the Palace as soon as they heard the news expressed joy and genuine delight. A huge full moon rose above the building as the crowds heard that new

Above: The world gets a long-awaited glimpse of new royal baby, Prince George.

father Prince William had said that he and Catherine 'could not be happier'. William's own father, Prince Charles, was proud to become a grandfather, while The Queen was 'delighted' to welcome her first great-grandson who will, one day, take his own place on the British throne.

THE PRINCE WHO WILL BE KING

Catherine and William spent the first night after the birth in their private suite at St Mary's with their newborn son. Unaware of the weight of history, past and present, on his tiny shoulders, the baby Prince slept peacefully. George will be the 43rd monarch since William the Conqueror won the English Crown at the Battle of Hastings in 1066 and he will eventually be the eighth monarch to descend from Queen Victoria.

Prince George, The Queen's third great-grandchild (but first great-grandson after Peter Phillips's girls, Savannah and Isla), will one day be Head of the Armed Forces, Supreme Governor of the Church of England, Head of State of 16 countries and, possibly, if the role continues, Head of the Commonwealth, which spans 54 nations worldwide and embraces more than two billion citizens.

Prince George's birth meant that for the first time since Queen Victoria's reign, when her great-grandson, the future Edward VIII, was born in 1894, the monarchy has three generations of heirs to the throne. In 1894 they were Queen Victoria's son Bertie, later Edward VII, his son, who became George V, and the ill-fated Edward VIII, who abdicated in 1936. Now the heirs are Prince Charles, heir presumptive Prince William and his son Prince George.

The Prince's birth was marked by two gun salutes, at Green Park and the Tower of London, while the bells of Westminster Abbey were rung in a celebratory peal lasting three hours and technical wizardry turned the splashing water in the Trafalgar Square fountains blue.

Of all the responses to this addition to the Royal Family, perhaps the most heartfelt was that of his grandfather, the Prince of Wales. The Prince – who is close to both his sons, William and Harry, playing an enormous part in their upbringing following the tragic death of their mother, Princess Diana – was clearly overwhelmed at the news.

'Both my wife and I are overjoyed at the arrival of my first grandchild,' said the Prince, who was in Yorkshire with his wife, the Duchess of Cornwall. 'Grandparenthood is a unique moment in anyone's life, as countless kind people have told me in recent months, so I am enormously proud and happy to be a grandfather for the first time,' he added.

The Prince of Wales, The Queen and the Duke of Edinburgh, the baby's maternal grandparents Carole and Michael Middleton, Prince Harry and other senior members of the Royal Family were the first to be told of Prince George's birth, before the public announcement was made.

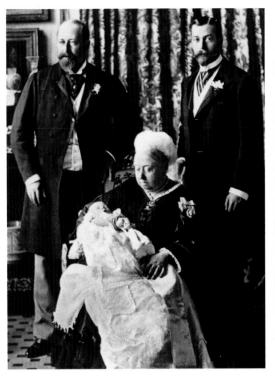

Left: Four generations of monarchs: Queen Victoria holds the baby who would later be King Edward VIII, on his christening day, 16 July 1894. The baby, dressed in the traditional beautiful Honiton lace christening gown, is flanked on either side by his grandfather (later Edward VII) and father (later George V).

Below: Kensington Palace, the London home of the Duke and Duchess of Cambridge and their children.

BRINGING UP A FUTURE KING

The Prime Minister, David Cameron, was sincere when he welcomed the 'wonderful moment for a warm and loving couple who have got a brand-new baby boy'.

The Duchess, in her early life as Kate Middleton, was brought up in a happy and caring family atmosphere by parents who worked hard to give her and her younger brother and sister the best childhood they could. Prince William's loving relationship with his mother, Princess Diana, was brought to an abrupt end when she died in 1997 at just 36 years old. But she had been a caring parent who loved her sons dearly, giving them the freedom and fun often denied to royal children in the past.

Like his father did, Prince George is enjoying as normal an upbringing as possible, with two parents determined to let him have as much privacy as possible. Although they want his early years to be comparatively free from protocol and formality, they know they have to balance this desire with a respect for royal tradition. Their son, after all, will one day be Head of State.

Baby George was taken home by his parents to Apartment 1A at Kensington Palace where the 20 rooms, once belonging to William's great-aunt, Princess Margaret, had been refurbished, with a large walled garden creating an ideal private playground.

There was much press debate as to whether George would be looked after by a nanny. Catherine and William wanted their son to experience the same family pleasures that Catherine and her siblings enjoyed, and planned to share childcare duties between

Left: William and Harry's nanny Jessie Webb, seen here with Michael Middleton, leaves the Chapel Royal in St James's Palace following the christening of Prince George.

Left: Full-time royal nanny to Prince George, Maria Teresa Turrion Borrallo.

them as much as possible, but it was always likely that a full-time nanny would be required. Initially they only hired Antonella Fresolone, previously The Queen's housemaid, as a general housekeeper, rather than appoint a nanny.

In September 2013, seven weeks after George's birth, it was reported that William's former nanny, Jessie Webb, had been invited out of retirement at the age of 71 to help the couple on a part-time basis. Miss Webb enjoyed a warm relationship with Princes William and Harry in the early 1990s, and William always stayed in touch with her, inviting her to both his 21st birthday party and his wedding.

With Miss Webb's help, and that of new grandmother Carole Middleton who has proved to be a key figure in George's life, the Duchess was able to return to some official duties. The young Prince is known to spend significant time at the Middleton's family home, a manor house with a tennis court, swimming pool and 18 acres in the quiet village of Bucklebury in Berkshire, where the young Catherine grew up and spent school holidays, away from Marlborough College.

In March 2014, a full-time Norland Nanny, from the famous Norland College in Bath where nannies have been trained since 1892, joined the royal household. Of the new recruit, Spanish-born Maria Teresa Turrion Borrallo, a spokesman said, 'The Duke and Duchess are of course delighted she has chosen to join them'. The timing was perfect, enabling Miss Borrallo to get to know her young charge before she travelled with the family on a tour of New Zealand and Australia in April 2014.

As well as the help of a nanny and the hands-on approach of his maternal grandparents, the influence of George's paternal grandparents is also a strong one, with summer holidays at Balmoral, with all the outdoor pleasures that the Royal Family's Scottish estate affords, and traditional family Christmases at Sandringham, in Norfolk.

The royal custom of home schooling was firmly broken when Diana sent her young sons, William and Harry, first to nursery school, then to Wetherby pre-preparatory school, before a time at Ludgrove School in Berkshire and then to Eton College, just a stone's throw from Windsor Castle.

Kate was educated at St Andrew's preparatory school in Berkshire, before boarding at Marlborough College. She and William met at St Andrews, Scotland's oldest university, when each studied there.

It is not yet known where the young Prince of Cambridge will be educated, but it is possible that one day he will become an Eton student, following his father and Uncle Harry who both have fond memories of their schooldays there.

Below: Harry looks to his big brother as the siblings are photographed on Harry's first day at Wetherby School, Notting Hill, where William had been a pupil for some time, in September 1989.

PRINCE GEORGE'S
CHRISTENING

Below: The Queen looks on fondly at her great-grandson in this official photograph of the immediate Royal Family at Prince George's christening on 23 October 2013.

Below right: As the Duchess of Cambridge carries Prince George, the Honiton lace royal christening gown is displayed to full effect.

Prince George made his second public appearance on the day of his christening, 23 October 2013, when he was three months old.

Breaking with a recent tradition of future monarchs being baptised at Buckingham Palace, the chosen venue was the Chapel Royal at St James's Palace. Princess Elizabeth, George's great-grandmother, was christened in a private chapel at Buckingham Palace – though, of course, at that time no one knew that her uncle, Edward VIII, would abdicate and she would one day be Queen. George's grandfather, Prince Charles, and father, Prince William, were both christened in the Music Room at Buckingham Palace.

As family and friends arrived at St James's Palace, all eyes were on Prince George. His lace and satin gown was handcrafted by Angela Kelly, one of The Queen's most trusted designers, and was a 2008 replica of the original royal christening gown fashioned from silk and Honiton lace that was first worn in 1841 by Queen Victoria's firstborn child, Victoria, the Princess Royal. Having been worn by over 60 royal babies during the course of more than 160 years it had, unsurprisingly, become very fragile. Viscount Severn, son of the Duke and Duchess of Wessex, first wore the Angela Kelly gown on his christening at Windsor Castle in April 2008.

Of course, there was much interest, too, in what new mother the Duchess of Cambridge would be wearing. The choice of outfits of Catherine and her sister, Pippa, complemented each other and toned perfectly with the christening gown. Catherine wore a knee-length cream ruffled suit by Alexander McQueen – the fashion house responsible for her wedding dress – which she accessorised with a matching hat by Jane Taylor and fashionably high heels; Pippa's cream coat was by British designer Suzannah Crabb.

Her Majesty The Queen was dressed in sky blue, her cashmere coat with mother-of-pearl buttons designed by Stewart Parvin. Her brooch was that given to her by her parents on the birth of Prince Charles in 1948. Camilla, Duchess of Cornwall, also went for an all-cream ensemble, with a bouclé coat and pearl necklace. Carole Middleton, George's grandmother, was elegant in a Catherine Walker navy blue coat with pretty lace panels, and hat by milliner Jane Corbett.

The ceremony was conducted by the Archbishop of Canterbury, the Most Reverend Justin Welby, who officially took the role of Archbishop on 4 February 2013, following the retirement of Dr Rowan Williams. In keeping with tradition, the Lily Font and water from the River Jordan were used for the baptism.

George's christening was an intimate affair with just 22 guests, mainly senior royals, the immediate members of the Middleton family and seven godparents (or sponsors as they are known in royal circles) and their spouses. Apart from Zara Tindall, Prince William's cousin, these were all friends of the Duke and Duchess of Cambridge: Oliver Baker, Earl Grosvenor (Hugh), Emilia Jardine-Paterson, Jamie Lowther-Pinkerton, Julia Samuel and William van Cutsem.

Left: The Duke of Cambridge arrives with Prince George for his christening at the Chapel Royal, St James's Palace.

Many royal children have been recipients of splendid christening presents. Soon after Princess Elizabeth was born in 1926, the chairman of the National Jewellers' Association arrived at the family home in Bruton Street bearing an exquisitely wrapped gift for the infant, made by members of his organisation. He said he hoped that the beautiful silver porringer, a small bowl with ivory handles carved to resemble thistles and a cover decorated with an ivory and silver coronet, would be placed upon 'the breakfast table of the first baby in the land'.

Right: In December 1984, Prince William kept everyone entertained during the official photographs at the christening of his brother, Prince Henry of Wales, known to the world as Prince Harry.

Below: The glorious Lily Font made in 1840–41 and used for royal christenings.

The service lasted 45 minutes. The hymns Prince George's parents chose were *Breathe on Me, Breath of God* and *Be Thou My Vision*. The two lessons, read by Pippa Middleton and Prince Harry, were taken from the gospels of St Luke and St John.

There were two anthems, *Blessed Jesus! Here We Stand* and *Lord Bless You and Keep You*, performed by the Choir of Her Majesty's Chapel Royal who also sang at William and Catherine's wedding.

Like the original royal christening gown, the magnificent silver-gilt Lily Font, made in 1840–41 and used for all royal baptisms, was commissioned by Queen Victoria for her daughter, Princess Victoria. When the font is not performing its intended role, it is kept with other royal treasures in the Tower of London.

The service over, the star of the show was whisked away to Clarence House where a private tea party hosted by the Prince of Wales and Duchess of Cornwall was held in his honour.

As is traditional for a firstborn, George's christening cake was a tier taken from William and Catherine's wedding cake. Similarly, in 1982 William's christening cake was a redecorated version of his parents' wedding cake. At Prince Charles's christening in 1948 the cake had three tiers. The first was from Princess Elizabeth and Prince Philip's wedding cake, decorated with intricate lace icing topped with a cradle in which was placed a baby doll, dressed in a magnificent robe sewn by members of the Royal Society of Art Needlework. The second tier was an enormous coronet-topped, three-foot-high cake, made by students from the National School of Bakery with ingredients contributed from countries of the British Empire. The third tier was given by the Universal Cookery and Food Association, and decorated with silver ornaments made by disabled silversmiths.

Christenings hold great significance for the Royal Family. It is a spiritually important event; a chance to give thanks to God for the gift of the child being baptised into the Christian faith. For Prince George there is added significance, as when he is eventually crowned he will carry the title Defender of the Faith and Supreme Governor of the Church of England.

Not all royal christenings have gone as smoothly as Prince George's. It is said that at Queen Victoria's christening in 1819 there was an unfortunate dispute about her name. Her German-born mother, Princess Victoria of Saxe-Coburg-Saalfeld, the Duchess of Kent, favoured Georgina Charlotte Augusta Alexandrina Victoria. Her father, Prince Edward, Duke of Kent and Strathearn, overruled his wife during the ceremony, insisting the baby be more simply named Alexandrina Victoria. Apparently the Duchess was so upset that she wept throughout the service.

2014–2015:
A GROWING FAMILY

In February 2014, with Prince William on a ten-week course in agricultural management at the University of Cambridge, with a view to helping him prepare for the role he will inherit from his father when he takes on the Duchy of Cornwall estate, Catherine was guest of honour at the National Portrait Gallery's Portrait Gala. Looking tanned and relaxed following a recent family holiday to Mustique, she wore a midnight-blue floor-length dress by Jenny Packham. In keeping with the dress code for the evening of 'black tie with a touch of sparkle', Catherine did indeed sparkle in a Nizam of Hyderabad diamond necklace, loaned to her by The Queen.

In April 2014 it was very much a family affair when the Duke and Duchess took their nine-month-old son with them on a three-week official tour of New Zealand and Australia. The Queen gave special permission for Prince William and Prince George to fly together, as usually two heirs to the throne would not do so; this was the same consent granted to Prince Charles when he and Princess Diana flew to Australia with nine-month-old William in 1983.

This was the first major public appearance of George since his christening, so his arrival in Wellington on 7 April after the 30-hour flight caused quite a stir. His parents fulfilled many

Right: An elegant Catherine arrives at the National Portrait Gallery, February 2014.

Far right: The Duke and Duchess of Cambridge arrive with Prince George in Wellington on the first day of their 2014 tour of New Zealand and Australia.

Black cocker spaniel Lupo, his name Italian for 'wolf', is very much part of the Cambridge family, given to Catherine by her parents in 2011 as an early Christmas present. He even stars in a book published in 2014: *The Adventures of Lupo the Royal Dog: The Secret of Windsor Castle* by Aby King.

Above: At Taronga Zoo in Sydney, William pets the bilby named George as Catherine and their son look on.

Right: A kiss and a cuddle from Prince William for Lupo, the family cocker spaniel, June 2014.

engagements in New Zealand before flying to Australia, arriving on 16 April for a further round of royal duties. With nanny Maria Teresa Turrion Borrallo on hand, their son was only seen on certain occasions during the royal visit, but stole the show every time, squealing with delight and wriggling in the arms of his mother or father, keen to get down and explore.

With their commitment to the conservation of wildlife, William and Catherine's visit to Taronga Zoo in Sydney was of particular significance, and one enjoyed by Prince George who was introduced to a bilby (a long-eared marsupial) named after him.

On 15 June 2014, several weeks before his first birthday, Prince George was seen toddling in public for the first time. He was with his mother at a charity polo match in Cirencester, Gloucestershire, supporting his father and Uncle Harry who were playing at the annual event. With Catherine holding his hand, George was sturdy on his feet – and he even showed his own sporting skills by kicking a football.

It is well known how much the Duke and Duchess of Cambridge value their privacy when not on royal duty, and how determined they are to protect their children from the glare of unauthorised publicity. However, with a first birthday being a special event, on 21 July, the day before Prince George's first birthday, new photographs of him were released, taken a few weeks previously at London's Natural History Museum, where the Duchess is patron. In a statement

Right: With his first birthday just a month away, on Father's Day 2014 Prince George attends Cirencester Park Polo Club to see his father and uncle play on opposing sides in the Jerudong Trophy charity polo match.

Far right: Like father, like son: it is easy to spot the family likeness in this photo of Prince William in the gardens of Kensington Palace on his first birthday in 1983.

that same day, the Duke and Duchess expressed thanks for the 'warm and generous good wishes' received on the occasion of their son's birthday.

On 22 July, the bells of Westminster Abbey rang out to mark the occasion, and avid royal fans placed balloons and flags outside Kensington Palace. However, royal celebrations were very much a private affair, with a tea party held for godparents and close family – minus Prince Charles and the Duchess of Cornwall who were undertaking a schedule of engagements in Scotland, where they are known as the Duke and Duchess of Rothesay.

News that the Duchess of Cambridge was pregnant with her second child came in September 2014. As with her first pregnancy, she was suffering from hyperemesis gravidarum (acute morning sickness) that often results in hospitalisation, so the couple decided to scotch rumours and make public her condition before the usual 12-week period.

In early December 2014, William and Catherine, minus baby George, had a three-day whistle-stop tour of the east coast of the United States. During their time there they visited the 9/11 memorial and museum, met with President Obama and watched a basketball game. Before flying home they attended a fundraising event for the university where they first met, St Andrews, at the Metropolitan Museum of Art in New York –

Left: Princess Elizabeth with Prince Charles on his first birthday, 14 November 1949. Like his son, William, and grandson, George, Charles was already walking by the time he turned one.

the first visit to the city for both of them. The Duchess looked timelessly elegant, her hair swept in a chignon and her gown offset with emerald drop earrings.

As a 'thank you' to the media for not publishing paparazzi images of Prince George, in mid-December 2014, just in time for Christmas, three new official photographs of their little boy were released. The photographs of the 16-month-old were taken in a courtyard at Kensington Palace the previous month.

As is tradition, Christmas morning 2014 saw hundreds of well-wishers gather to see The Queen and other members of the Royal Family arrive for a service at St Mary Magdalene church at Sandringham. The Duke and Duchess of Cambridge walked hand-in-hand to the church, joined by the Duchess's parents and younger siblings who were staying with them on the Sandringham Estate. Prince George, considered too young to sit still in church, had been left with his nanny.

Looking after an energetic two-year-old is great fun but when you are pregnant it can be very tiring, so it was undoubtedly fortunate that Carole Middleton was able to step in and help during the latter stages of her daughter's pregnancy.

To enable William and Catherine to have family time together, Carole ensured the day-to-day maintenance of their Norfolk home ran like clockwork. Mr Middleton, too, played his part, in particular busying himself around the substantial grounds.

With her parents' support behind the scenes, Catherine maintained a busy schedule in the lead-up to her due date. In early March 2015 she attended the reopening of The Goring Hotel, an occasion that also marked the London hotel's 105th anniversary. The Goring holds a special place in Catherine's heart as it was here that she and her close family and friends spent the night before her wedding. Dressed in a vibrant floral dress by Erdem, the Duchess showed off her artistic talent when she added a final flourish to the hand-painted wallpaper in the front hall, the final part of the hotel's renovations. She had previously revealed that Prince George

Below: William and Catherine leave St Paul's Cathedral following a service commemorating troops who were stationed in Afghanistan, March 2015.

Right: The Goring Hotel – where the Duchess of Cambridge spent the night before her wedding in 2011 and where, in 2015, she attended its reopening following a major refurbishment – was awarded a Royal Warrant in 2013 in recognition of its services to the Royal Family.

On 13 March 2015, senior royals – including William and Catherine – attended a service at St Paul's Cathedral, led by Her Majesty The Queen, to mark the end of combat operations in Afghanistan. Prince Harry, himself an Afghan veteran who completed two tours of duty there, joined the 2,600-strong congregation, many of whom were there to honour loved ones who lost their lives during the conflict. Just four days later it was announced that Harry would leave the army in June. Although he admitted it had been a 'really tough decision' after ten years of service, he said he is looking forward to a 'new chapter' in his life.

Below: Prince William, dressed in a traditional Japanese yukata, sits opposite Japan's Prime Minister Shinzo Abe and shares a joke with him as they dine at a hot spring inn in Koriyama, Fukushima, February 2015.

was showing an interest in painting, an activity they enjoy together, while William has made it known that their son, like many toddlers today, enjoys playing games on an iPad.

In the meantime, William was on an official visit to Asia. He arrived in Tokyo on 26 February, the first leg of a week-long tour through Japan and China. At the historic Hama Rikyu gardens, he took part in a traditional green tea ceremony performed by a Grand Master, sipping from an antique Korean bowl.

Prince William is the most senior British royal to visit China since The Queen's tour of the country in 1986. On his last day there, he spoke at the Xishuangbanna Elephant Sanctuary, condemning trade in illegal wildlife and saying that China can be a global leader in the fight against it; he also praised the country for its contribution to the protection of wildlife in Africa.

While William was on tour, he learned that he had passed the exams to qualify as an air ambulance pilot, in plenty of time to begin his new role later in 2015 with the East Anglian Air Ambulance service, covering shifts for the teams based in both Cambridge and Norwich.

Left: During his 2015 visit to China, Prince William feeds a carrot to Ran Ran, a female elephant rescued by the Xishuangbanna Elephant Sanctuary ten years previously.

Left: The Duchess of Cambridge chats to *Downton Abbey* actors Sophie McShera (who plays Daisy Mason) and Lesley Nicol (Mrs Patmore) during a visit to the set of the programme at Ealing Studios in March 2015, just seven weeks before the birth of her daughter.

On 12 March 2015, the Duchess of Cambridge made one of her final public appearances before the arrival of her second child when she visited Ealing Studios in London where much of the filming of the TV drama *Downton Abbey* takes place. A fan of the programme, she met some of the cast from both upstairs and below stairs, including Michelle Dockery, who plays Lady Mary Crawley, and Jim Carter, *Downton*'s butler Mr Carson, who said the Duchess was 'very enthusiastic' about the series and 'knew all about it'.

THE NEW ARRIVAL

On Saturday 2 May 2015 the nation received the news it had been waiting for: that the second child of the Duke and Duchess of Cambridge had arrived safely. And, as many had hoped, the baby was a girl.

With the general election campaign in full swing and taking up much news coverage, the media was nevertheless on tenterhooks waiting to hear that the Duchess had gone into labour. It was a long wait. Although the due date of the new baby was never announced publicly, it was generally understood that the latest addition to the Royal Family was expected to arrive mid to late April, and was certainly overdue when she held out until May.

Wanting to avoid a media circus, the Duke and Duchess had requested that the press and public not be permitted to wait outside St Mary's Hospital, Paddington in the weeks approaching the birth. With security barriers erected and parking restrictions in place, reporters

Below: The announcement outside Buckingham Palace of the safe arrival of the Princess of Cambridge on 2 May 2015.

Right: The Duke and Duchess of Cambridge greet the crowds outside the hospital with their baby daughter, less than ten-hours after she was born.

were instead permitted their own corralled area. However, as April provided many mild, sunny days in southern England, several die-hard royal fans were not deterred and camped out on the pavement, determined to be there when the news was finally announced.

When Catherine's time came, it all happened pretty quickly. The Duchess was admitted to the Lindo Wing of St Mary's Hospital early on the morning of 2 May, and Britain awoke to learn that she was in labour. Soon after 11 a.m. came the news: that she had been delivered of her second child, a daughter, at 8.34 a.m.. Weighing in at 8lb 3oz, Prince George's little sister is just 3oz lighter than he was at birth.

With Prince William in attendance, the delivery was overseen by Guy Thorpe-Beeston, a consultant obstetrician and surgeon-gynaecologist to the royal household, and Alan Farthing, who had assisted Sir Marcus Setchell at Prince George's birth. In stark contrast to his sister's speedy arrival, George's delivery had taken over ten hours.

The media had received the news of the birth of the new Princess shortly before it appeared on Twitter, direct from Kensington Palace. It was another 90 minutes before the easel with the declaration about the birth was erected outside Buckingham Palace, the traditional honour bestowed on this occasion to footmen George Oates and Simon Garnett. London landmarks got in on the act too, with Tower Bridge glowing pink and the neon billboard around the Post Office Tower scrolling 'It's a girl'.

Shortly before 4 o'clock, Prince William – stopping just long enough to tell the waiting crowds that 'we're very, very happy' – dashed home to Kensington Palace to collect Prince George. Arriving back at the hospital with his son 15 minutes later, the small boy dressed all in blue and so rarely seen in public looked a little bemused by the cheering crowds and ranks of photographers, and was scooped into his father's arms. Encouraged by William, George managed an uncertain wave before disappearing into the building where his mother and new sister were waiting for him.

Right: Flanked by the Duke of Edinburgh and the Duke of York, The Queen was dressed all in pink on the day her newest great-granddaughter was born.

Below: Looking happy and relaxed, William and Catherine share a smile as they introduce their daughter to the world.

George had been already been taken home, via a rear entrance at the hospital, when at around 6 p.m., just 12 hours after they first arrived, his parents emerged to proudly show the world their new daughter. It was difficult to believe that Catherine, looking fresh as a daisy, had given birth only that morning. Dressed in a white dress adorned with yellow flowers by designer Jenny Packham and nude high-heels, she looked as elegant as ever.

Whilst her parents smiled and waved to the crowds, their little girl – as yet unnamed – slept on, blissfully unaware of the excitement her arrival had created. Wrapped in a white woollen shawl by G.H. Hurt & Son, her head was kept warm and cosy against the chill spring wind in a cream knitted bonnet.

With his wife and daughter settled in the car and ready to set off for home, Prince William held up two fingers in acknowledgement that he was now father of two. The happy smiles of the Duke and Duchess as they drove off told the world how happy they are to have become parents again. Happy, too, were their families.

The Queen, attending an official engagement at Richmond in North Yorkshire with her second son, the Duke of York, beamed when congratulated on her newest great-granddaughter; and surely it was no coincidence that Her Majesty was dressed from head to toe in pink that day? Grandfather Prince Charles, who had earlier that week revealed he was hoping for a granddaughter, and the Duchess of Cornwall were 'absolutely delighted'. It is

Six months prior to Prince George's birth, The Queen overturned a 1917 decree that meant if William and Catherine's firstborn had been a daughter she would have been known as Lady, rather than Her Royal Highness. A Letters Patent issued by King George V had limited titles within the Royal Family, meaning that only a firstborn son would automatically become a prince, and excluded all future sons and daughters from a similar title. However, the new declaration states that 'all the children of the eldest son of the Prince of Wales should have and enjoy the style, title and attribute of royal highness with the titular dignity of Prince or Princess prefixed to their Christian names or with such other titles of honour'.

Above: Just hours old, the Princess of Cambridge sleeps peacefully throughout her first introduction to the press.

understood that they met the baby for the first time at Kensington Palace the day after she was born, as did Catherine's parents. Prince Harry, in the meantime, was in Australia on secondment to the Australian army.

The new baby's names were announced on 4 May as Charlotte Elizabeth Diana. Whilst the names given to both George and Charlotte were made known just two days after they were born, the names of their paternal grandfather were not made public until the day of his christening, a full month after his birth: Charles Philip Arthur George. Their father, too, was unnamed when he left hospital with a nametag identifying him only as 'Baby Wales'. It was a week before his names became known: William Arthur Philip Louis.

With many hoping that the new baby would be a girl, there had been much speculation that she would be named Elizabeth Diana. However, the most popular name, according to bookmakers, was Alice, with Charlotte and Victoria being close contenders. Had the baby been a second son, amongst bookmakers' favoured names were Spencer, the family name of Prince William's mother, Diana. When the new baby's names were announced, the Earl of Spencer, Princess Charlotte's great uncle and Diana's brother, was thrilled; his youngest child, born in 2012, is Lady Charlotte Diana.

Prince Charles is also sure to be delighted that his granddaughter is called Charlotte, the female version of his own name, which has long had royal connections. Charlotte has been a popular name since the 18th century when George III married Princess Charlotte of Mecklenburg-Strelitz in 1761. Although the marriage was a political one – the couple did not meet until their wedding day – the pair made a good match, and it was for her that the King purchased Buckingham House (now Buckingham Palace) as a family retreat.

On the arrival of their latest grandchild, it was anticipated that Mr and Mrs Middleton would move into Anmer Hall for the first six weeks to give William – expected to be on paternity leave until early June – and Catherine their support, and to help ensure that Prince George's routine would not be unduly disrupted with his new sister in residence.

Until 1990, Anmer Hall, situated two miles from the main house on the Sandringham Estate, had been the home of the Duke and Duchess of Kent for nearly 30 years. For ten years it was leased to Hugh and Emilie van Cutsem, who later made their home on their estate in Norfolk. Hugh, who died in 2013, and Prince Charles formed a long-lasting friendship when they were at Cambridge University together. Princes William and Harry became great friends of the van Cutsems' four sons, and knew Anmer Hall well while they were growing up. Charles is godfather to Edward van Cutsem, a pageboy at his wedding to Lady Diana Spencer. William is godfather to Grace van Cutsem – the bridesmaid much-photographed at his wedding when she covered her ears on the balcony of Buckingham Palace during the military fly-past.

In 2013 planning permission for Anmer Hall was granted, enabling work to commence on making internal changes and improving the security system, creating a country home for the Duke and Duchess of Cambridge and their family.

Her Royal Highness Princess Charlotte of Cambridge is The Queen's fifth great-grandchild. Peter Phillips and his wife, Autumn, were first to present Her Majesty with a child of this next generation when Savannah was born on 29 December 2010, followed by her sister, Isla, on 29 March 2012. Next came Prince George on 22 July 2013, followed by Zara and Michael Tindall's daughter, Mia, on 17 January 2014. However, this cannot compare to Queen Victoria: she and Prince Albert had nine children and 42 grandchildren, who between them gave Victoria an astonishing 87 great-grandchildren.

The daughter of the Duke and Duchess of Cambridge is the first baby to take the title Princess of Cambridge since George III's granddaughter, born in 1833, and is the most senior princess born since Princess Anne in 1950. In fact there has not been a new princess in the Royal Family for 25 years, since the birth of Princess Eugenie, youngest daughter of the Duke and Duchess of York. Eugenie's elder sister, Princess Beatrice, has moved to seventh place in the order of succession and, significantly for her, by law only the first six in line to the throne have to ask The Queen's permission to marry.

Above: Buckingham Palace was originally purchased by King George III for his Queen, Princess Charlotte of Mecklenburg-Strelitz, as a comfortable family home close to their official royal residence, St James's Palace.

Like her great-grandmother, her grandfather, her father and elder brother, all the main events in the new Princess Charlotte's life will be documented by the media. Her birth, christening, first day at school, sporting achievements and all the ups and downs of life are events in which the world will take more than a little interest. And, being a child of the 21st century, this will be with the added pressures that social media brings.

As with Prince George, though, Charlotte's parents will ensure their new daughter will enjoy as normal an upbringing as possible. They want the same for their children that all loving parents desire – that they grow to be happy and healthy. Despite the fact that both their children will ultimately play an official role in the Royal Family, William and Catherine will ensure that George and Charlotte are protected from the pressures of public duty for as long as possible.

A FUTURE TOGETHER

Although the news of the impending arrival of a second child for the Duke and Duchess of Cambridge caused international excitement, it created less of a stir than the announcement of Catherine's first pregnancy and its constitutional significance. Princess Charlotte is fourth in line to the throne, but, God willing, she is not destined to be monarch. Instead, she will be in the same position as Prince William's younger brother, Prince Harry. With first-hand knowledge of what it is like to be 'the back-up' (as Harry's mother, Diana, Princess of Wales jokingly and affectionately referred to him), there is little doubt that Princess Charlotte will have an ally in Uncle Harry; there is no one better placed to understand what it means to be the younger sibling of an heir to the throne.

It may be a long while yet before William becomes king. It has long been known that his grandmother, Queen Elizabeth II, has no desire to abdicate. Although in recent times she has gradually called on younger members of the Royal Family to share more of her duties, for someone celebrating their 90th birthday in 2016 she still fulfils an extraordinarily demanding role with an energy that belies her years.

Prince Charles, The Queen's heir, is destined to have a short reign, but reign he surely will. William certainly has no wish for his father to stand aside in his favour, with a royal spokesperson saying in 2010 that there was no question in William's mind that Charles will be the next monarch, and that the Duke of Cambridge 'has no desire to climb the ladder of kingship before his time'.

William wants a chance to enjoy family life before becoming Head of State. This young man has long been 'the people's prince', combining the informal, accessible personality and winning smile for which his mother was so well loved with his father's steady gaze, engaging conviction and quiet sensitivity.

Despite having many of the best qualities of both his parents, William, it seems, models himself most closely on his grandmother. As he told royal biographer Robert Hardman, Her Majesty does not care for celebrity. Her grandson knows that with the privileges afforded to him as part of the monarchy he has to set examples, doing what he calls 'one's duty', serving the country and using his position for the good.

Since William and Catherine's marriage, the popularity of the Royal Family has only increased. This good-humoured, handsome couple are well aware of their responsibilities – not only as parents but also to the nation. If their success at pleasing the public at home and abroad during royal duties and tours thus far is anything to go by, they will weather the storm of publicity that follows them wherever they go in determined style, protecting their private lives and raising two happy children in a warm, loving and united family environment.

Opposite: Two future kings: a tender moment between father and son, Prince William and Prince George.

ACKNOWLEDGEMENTS

Acknowledgement is made to Annie Bullen, author of *William & Catherine: A Royal Wedding Souvenir* (Pitkin Publishing, 2011) and *Royal Babies* (Pitkin Publishing, 2013), from which some chapters of *William and Catherine: A Family Portrait* have been adapted.

All photographs by kind permission of:
Press Association Images: FC (Dominic Lipinski/PA Wire); pp1, 3, 26, 39t, 44, 46r, 47 (John Stillwell/PA Wire); p2, BC (Daniel Leal-Olivas/PA Wire); p6 (Duncan Raban/ EMPICS Entertainment); pp7t, 13tr, 20m, 24t, 39bl, 48t, 52tr (Anwar Hussein/EMPICS Entertainment); p7b Suzanne Plunkett/PA Wire; pp8, 27, 37b (Arthur Edwards/The Sun/PA Wire); pp9, 50r, 51l, 55b, 63 (Chris Jackson/PA Wire); p12 (AP Photo/John Redman); pp13tl, 14, 15b, 52b (PA Archive); p15t (Toby Melville/PA Archive); p16l (Ben Gurr/The Times/NPA rota); p16r (AP Photo/Julian Smith); p17t (AP Photo/Sang Tan); p18 (Frank May/DPA); p19 (Paul Hilton/Demotix); p20l (Michael Dunlea/Daily Mail/PA Archive); p21t (AP Photo/Jon Super); p21b (Doug Peters/EMPICS Entertainment); p22 (Ken Jack/Demotix); p24b (Michael Dunlea/Anwar Hussein Collection); p25 (Harry Page/PA Wire); p29 (AP Photo/Kirsty Wigglesworth); pp28, 45b (Ron Bell/PA Archive); p36 (Kevin Lim/AP Images); p37t (JMP/ ABACA); p38 (Patrick van Katwijk/DPA); p39br (Sean Dempsey/PA Wire); pp40 both, 41tr, 41br, 41bl, 42 (PA Images); pp45t, 57b (Anthony Devlin/PA Wire); p48b (PA Archive/© H.M. Queen); p49 (Tim Ireland/PA Wire); p50l (Olivia Harris/WPA Rota); p53bl (Joe O'Brien/ Demotix); p53br (Lefteris Pitarakis/AP Images); p54 (Yomiuri/AP Images); p55t (AP Images); p56bl (Steve Parsons/PA Wire); p57t (Yui Mok/PA Wire); p58t (John Giles/PA Wire); p59 (Matt Crossick/EMPICS Entertainment).
Alamy: p13b (Trinity Mirror/Mirrorpix).
Getty Images: pp20b, 23b, 23t, 30, 31 both, 33 both, 34, 35, 41tl, 56br, 58b; p17b (Christopher Furlong/WPA Pool); pp51r, 52tl (Max Mumby/Indigo).
Bridgeman: p43t (Private Collection/The Stapleton Collection/Bridgeman Images).
Pitkin Publishing: pp43b, 61 (Heather Hook).
Camera Press: p46l (Jason Bell).